iOS 7
The 'Just What You Need' Book

What's New in iOS 7 for the iPhone® and iPad®

Galen Gruman

iOS 7:The "Just What You Need" Book

Published by The Zango Group, www.zangogroup.com/books.html

ISBN: 978-1492312635

Editor: Carol Person

Colophon: This book was produced using the ITC Giovanni typeface for the body text, Gill Sans for the chapter titles and subheads, and ITC Eras for the sidebar text, tip text, and caption text.

Contents

Contents

 Contacts

 Reminders

  Maps

  Videos

 Camera

 Photo Booth

 Photos

 Game Ce

 Messages

 Clock

 App Store

 iTunes St

 alculator

 The Weather Channel
TWC

 Find Friends

 FaceTir

● ● ● ● ● ● ●

  Friday 9

Introduction

t's hard to believe that there's an iOS 7 already. Or that the iPhone debuted just six years ago, and the iPad just three. They have changed mobile computing — in fact, all computing — so profoundly despite their youth. But here we are.

iOS 7 is a radical reinvention of the operating system used in the iPhone, iPad, and iPod Touch. The look and feel are very different: bold, stripped-down, young, and "flat" have all been used to describe it. No doubt, the new look and feel will be disconcerting for many users, as it gets rid of the details such as shadows, real-world analogies, and dimensionality that iOS has had since the beginning.

The focus on essentials is part of a larger design trend; Windows Phone is the most notable example of it in the mobile world, but Google has long taken this approach in its search engine. So perhaps it was just a matter of time before Apple, the current granddaddy of mobile, decided to adopt this fresher design trend.

No matter why — it's here. It took me only about a month of using iOS 7 before my mind made the switch and started looking at iOS 6 as "old." I believe you'll adapt quickly, too.

And once you get past the very different look, you'll find that iOS works very much like it always has. The gestures are the same, for example, and so are key interface notions like having app home screens, the app dock, and the status bar. Your existing apps will run just fine in the new interface, even if new ones begin to take on the new look and the new visual interactions among elements, such as the extensive use of overlays, motion, and "physics," meaning the use of perspective and relative size as objects interact.

There are of course new capabilities in iOS 7, but they mostly build on what you already know. So iOS 7 is both radically new and comfortingly familiar. That's important for iPhone and iPad owners, because nearly all of you will update to iOS 7 quickly, whether you keep your existing device or get a new one. That's why, rather than repeat all the details on the iOS you already know and use, I created this book to focus on what's new and different, so you can quickly take advantage of iOS 7's enhancements. That's the whole notion of the *iOS 7: The "Just What You Need" Book.*

If you're new to iOS, I can recommend several good books that will give you the full picture. My own Exploring iPad For Dummies has 166 pages of details on iOS and its main applications in the context of the iPad. To order it online, go to http://amzn.to/18tPUZc. (Alas, there is no iOS 7-specific version of that book.) For a solid introduction to the iPhone, consider getting David Pogue's iPhone: The Missing Manual. To order it online, go to http://amzn.to/1e2al5A.

Turn the page to start your journey to what's new in iOS 7!

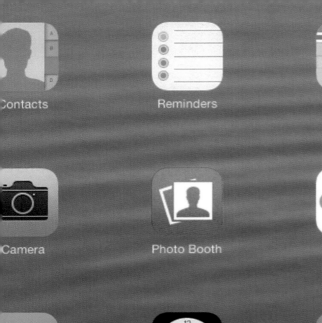

Contacts

Reminders

Maps

Video:

Camera

Photo Booth

Photos

Game Ce

lessages

Clock

App Store

iTunes S

alculator

The
Weather
Channel

TWC

Find Friends

FaceTir

● ● ● ● ● ● ●

Friday

9

Basic Interface

OS7 makes your iPhone, iPod Touch, or iPad look really, really different. The fonts, icons, color schemes, application borders, and controls all look different from how they looked in all previous iOS versions. But don't panic: iOS 7 operates very much like the previous versions, despite the new look.

The new look simplifies the screen and its elements, providing more space for applications' content and providing a clean, crisp, more modern look. Largely gone are the real-world analogs (a technique known as *skeuomorphism*), replaced with spare, often sketch-like representations that rely more on simulated physics such as relative motion and scale to represent where to focus and what is occurring. iOS 7 also favors text over icons in controls, though both are used; the emphasis on text labels reduces ambiguity about your options, an issue icons can present.

You'll also see extensive use of overlays on screens rather than windows, pop-overs, or new screens. Figure 1-1 shows an example of Siri's new overlay look, which leaves whatever you were viewing or working on somewhat visible in the background. (I describe some of Siri's new capabilities Chapter 2.)

No matter what apps you use, you can expect them to look different because of the revamped user interface. In most cases, all that has

■ FIGURE 1-1
iOS 7 uses overlays extensively, as shown here for Siri.

changed is the look. This book looks at new or changed functions in iOS itself and in the default apps that Apple includes. This chapter helps you make the mental transition from the old interface cues to the new look.

 Note

Throughout this book, you can assume that when I mention the iPhone, what I write also applies to the iPod Touch. Except of course for iPhone-only features such as its LED flash and its ability to make and receive phone calls.

New Look and Behaviors for the Home Screen

Let's start with the home screen, where the new look is most evident: The typeface is thinner but clearer, the icons and badges are simplified and "flat" (without the 3-D effects of previous iOS versions), and the dock has a cleaner background, as Figure 1-2 shows.

The signal-strength indicator for cellular connections in the status bar at top has also changed to a row of dots. When the battery is being charged, a plus sign (+) appears to the right of the battery icon.

■ FIGURE 1-2

The home screen for the iPad and iPhone.

You may notice that when you swipe the home screen to the leftmost position, you no longer get the Search screen. That's because the Search screen is gone. Instead, you pull down on the current screen (be sure to drag outside any app icons) to reveal the Search bar, as Figure 1-3 shows. Except for how you access it, the Search bar works as before.

■ FIGURE 1-3

The Search bar no longer appears in its own screen.

A more radical change is the multitasking dock in iOS 7. When you double-press the Home button (or do a four-finger swipe up on the iPad), you no longer see the familiar dock and the current app or home

■ FIGURE 1-4

The multitasking dock is replaced with the multitasking screen, which also shows a preview window of what's currently running in each open or recently open app.

■ FIGURE 1-5

To quit an app, drag it up from the multitasking screen and toss it up and away.

screen pushed up. Instead, in the new multitasking screen, you see a row of open windows in the center and the app icons below, as Figure 1-4 shows. Scroll sideways to move through the apps. As before, the apps are organized so the most recently opened app is at the far left and the least

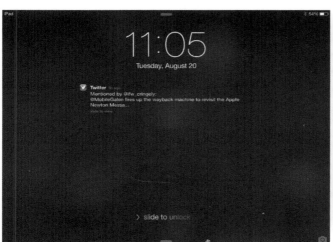

☐ FIGURE 1-6

The lock screen for the iPad and iPhone.

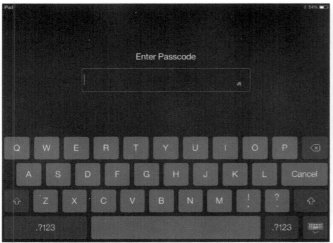

☐ FIGURE 1-7

The sign-in screen for the iPad and iPhone.

■ FIGURE 1-8

The lock screen for the iPad and iPhone with and without the playback controls

recently opened one is at the far right. Tap a screen or its icon to switch to that app.

As before, tap the Home button to close the multitasking screen. Also as before, you can use a four-finger side swipe to navigate among open apps on the iPad, as long as you are using an app rather than viewing a home screen.

Quitting an app also changes in the new multitasking view. Before, you tapped and held an app icon in the multitasking dock to cause the icons to wiggle and the Close button (the – symbol) to appear on each

◼ FIGURE 1-9

The lock screen shows any timer in progress below the current time (at left), as well as the control to mute the alarm once the timer completes (at right).

icon, then you tapped the Close button on an app icon to quit it. Now, as Figure 1-5 shows, you drag an app's window to the top of the screen to toss it out, which causes the app's window and icon to disappear and the app to quit.

New Look and Behaviors for the Lock Screen

Likewise, the lock screen has also been simplified, with the top and bottom bars gone, as shown in Figure 1-6. As Figure 1-7 shows, the sign-in screen also has a simpler look, and sporting the new keyboard design (if your password is not just numerals, that is). The keyboard color varies in iOS 7 based on what's behind it, rather than be the all-black look of before.

If music is playing, you can toggle the lock screen between showing the time in large numerals and showing the playback controls, as Figure 1-8 shows — just as in previous versions of iOS. But what's different is that it now takes just a single press of the Home button to switch between the two views, not a double-press as before.

Also, when you have a timer going in the Clock app, its status now displays in the lock screen, as Figure 1-9 shows, so you don't have to fumble to unlock the device and then go to the Clock app.

□ FIGURE 1-10

The Control Center takes playback, screen-brightness, mute, and rotation lock controls that used to be in the multitasking dock and adds quick-access buttons to control network connections, AirDrop, and Do Not Disturb mode, and to open several handy utilities.

The New Control Center

One completely new capability in iOS 7 is the Control Center, a tray of commonly used functions you can access from the home screens, the lock screen, and apps. Swipe up from the bottom of the screen to open it; Figure 1-10 shows the Control Center. Swipe its handle down to close the Control Center.

○ Tip

If you find yourself opening the Control Center by accident in apps, you can disable it in the Settings app's Control Center pane. Set the Access within Apps switch to Off. You can also disable the Control Center in the lock screen by setting the Access on Lock Screen switch to Off.

○ Note

On the iPad, a short rounded line at the bottom of the screen indicates that you can access the Control Center by swiping up from its approximate location. This visual cue does not display on the iPhone.

The capabilities vary a bit depending on the device you have. Older iPhones and iPads don't have the hardware needed to run the AirDrop feature (explained Chapter 2). And the AirPlay control won't appear if there's no AirPlay-compatible device in range. Also, iPhones have the Flashlight and Calculator buttons that the iPad does not because current iPads don't have LEDs in the cameras and don't have the Calculator app.

The Control Center takes the playback, brightness, and AirPlay controls that used to exist in the now-defunct multitasking dock (if you swiped all the way to the left) and adds new controls. Here's what it does:

- **Playback controls:** You get the Play/Pause, Rewind, and Fast-Forward buttons and Volume slider of the old multitasking dock, plus a scrubber bar to advance the playback and the name of the current album and song that is playing, the current podcast and episode that is playing, or the name of the movie or TV show that is playing. If you're playing a podcast, you also get the 30-second skip controls of the Podcast app.

- **AirPlay control:** The AirPlay button appears if an AirPlay device is detected on the network.

- **Lock and mute controls:** You get either the Rotation Lock or Mute button of the old multitasking dock. If you set the side switch in the Settings app to control muting, the Control Center shows the Rotation Lock button; if you set the side switch in the Settings app to control rotation lock, the Control Center shows the Mute button

- **Screen-brightness control:** You get the Screen Brightness slider of the old multitasking dock.

- **AirDrop control:** This new button lets you set your visibility to other iOS devices for sharing via AirDrop; the choices are Off, Contacts Only, and Everyone.

- **Networking controls:** New to iOS 7 are three buttons that people have long wanted quick access to. They are Airplane Mode, Wi-Fi, and Bluetooth. You can quickly turn off or on the device's radios without having to go to the Settings app. (You can still turn them on or off there, and you continue to select your Wi-Fi networks in the Settings app and pair Bluetooth devices in Settings.)

- **Utility access:** Also new to iOS 7 are the quick-access buttons for launching the Clock and Camera apps on both iPads and iPhones, plus the Flashlight and Calculator buttons on iPhones. Tapping Calculator launches the Calculator app, while tapping

Flashlight turns on the LED so your phone can act as a flashlight (tap it again to turn off the LED).

■ **Do Not Disturb control:** There's also a new button to enable or disable Do Not Disturb mode, which silences alerts from people based on the settings established in the Settings app's Do Not Disturb pane. Before, you had to open the Settings app to manually enable or disable Do Not Disturb.

The Expanded Notification Center

The Notification Center — the pull-down tray of recent e-mails, tweets, appointments, texts, and other alerts — has gotten a major makeover in iOS 7. He big change is that there are now three screens you can switch among in the Notification Center by using the buttons at the top.

There's still the original screen, now called All, shown in Figure 1-11.

But there is also the Missed screen, which shows you only alerts you have not seen, rather than show the history of your alerts that the All screen provide. Like All, you can delete alerts by tapping the Delete icon (the X in a circle) to the right of the alert. The Close button is much more visible in iOS 7 than it had been in previous versions.

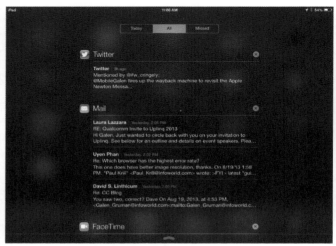
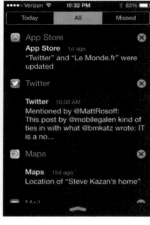

■ FIGURE 1-11

The All screen in the Notification Center provides the alerts history familiar from previous iOS versions.

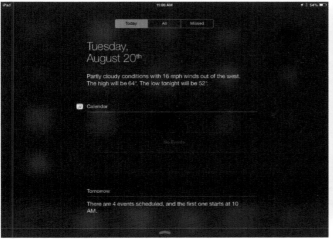

■ FIGURE 1-12

The Today screen in the Notification Center shows your day's schedule, the current weather forecast, and a summary of tomorrow's schedule.

◎ Note

On the iPad, a short rounded line at the top of the screen indicates that you can access the Notification Center by swiping down from its approximate location. This visual cue does not display on the iPhone.

The third screen, Today, summarizes your day, displaying your calendar, as well as a summary of the weather at top and a summary of your next day's calendar at bottom, as Figure 1-12 shows. The Today screen often can't hold all the details, so be sure to scroll down to see if any more information is available.

The Settings app's Notification Center pane (called Notifications in prior iOS version) adds several new switches to control what appears in the Notification Center. For the lock screen you can set whether the Notifications view (what appears in the Notification Center's All screen) and whether the Today view display. For the Notification Center's Today view, you can specify which of the following display: the weather forecast (the Today Summary switch), the calendar (the Calendar Day View switch), reminders (from the Reminders app), and the summary of tomorrow's schedule. On the iPhone, there's an additional switch to set whether stock data appears; it pulls in the current data for the stocks you track in the Stocks app.

Contacts

Reminders

Maps

Video

Camera

Photo Booth

Photos

Game Ce

Messages

Clock

App Store

iTunes S

Calculator

TWC

Find Friends

FaceTi

○ ● ○ ○ ○ ○ ○

Friday
9

Apps and Common Services

Before I explain changes in the apps that Apple includes with iOS 7 (in Chapters 3 through 6), it's important to understand the changes that you'll find across all apps, as well as the common services that iOS offers, such as Share sheets and Siri.

New Looks for Apps and Their Controls

The new "flat" design means that the icons for many apps — and certainly all those from Apple — change in iOS 7, so you can expect a period of adjustment to find the apps you want. Table 2-1 compares the iOS 6 and iOS 7 app icons to help you make the mental switch.

Within apps, you'll see the same new font (Helvetica Neue) and "flat" look as on the home screen, as well as fewer borders around content — that gives apps more breathing space and a cleaner look.

Also, within apps, some of the controls also look very different. For example, the selection dial for times and dates is strikingly different, losing the look of a physical wheel, as Figure 2-1 shows. But you still scroll the "wheel" as before to choose the desired entry.

Folders also look different, using as Figure 2-2 shows a rounded rectangle to hold app icons rather than the screen-split look of before. But it behaves the same.

Table 2-1: The new icons for Apple's built-in iOS apps

APP	iOS 7 ICON	PREVIOUS ICON
App Store		
Calculator		
Calendar	Thursday 29	Thursday 29
Camera		
Clock		
Compass		
Contacts		
FaceTime		
Game Center		
iTunes Store		
Mail		
Maps	280	280
Messages		
Music		

APP	IOS 7 ICON	PREVIOUS ICON
Newsstand		
Notes		
Passbook		
Phone		
Photo Booth		
Photos		
Reminders		
Safari		
Settings		
Stocks		
Videos		
Voice Memos		
Weather		

The icons for several common controls have also changed, as Table 2-2 shows. These are used mainly in Mail and Safari, but you'll see them in other apps as well.

Table 2-2: The new icons for Apple's common controls

CONTROL	IOS 7 ICON	PREVIOUS ICON
Back		
Bookmark		
Flag		
Forward		
iCloud/Photo Stream		
Move to Folder		
New (message)		
New (tab or window)		
Reply		
Share		
Trash		

Another change in iOS 7 is one you'll see only gradually. Apple has added a control for text size in the Settings app's General pane. The Text Size slider, shown in Figure 2-3, lets you set the default size for text in applications. But the catch is that apps have to be written to take advantage of this feature, so it may be a while before all your apps adapt their presentation to your settings here. But you can see it in action now in Apple apps like Mail.

iOS 7 changes the button that appears when you flick left on an item such as a mail message in a list. Typically, you got the Delete button in previous versions of iOS. Now, you get the Delete or Trash button, which has a bolder look, and often a More button as well, as

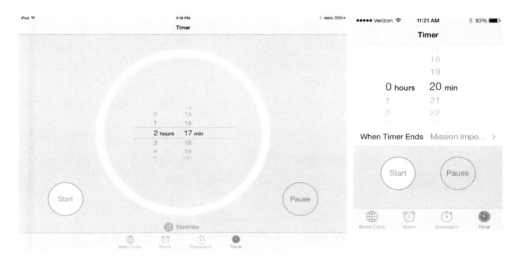

■ FIGURE 2-1
The new selection wheel dispenses with the look of a physical wheel.

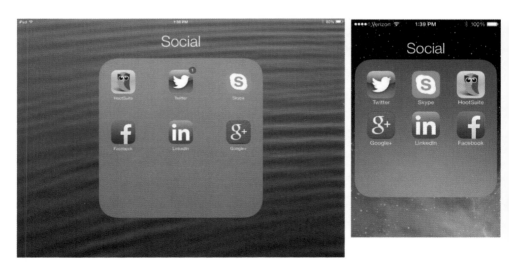

■ FIGURE 2-2
The app folder has a new look but behaves the same as before.

Figure 2-4 shows. Tap More to get additional options, such as Mark as Unread and Move to Trash in Mail or the details screen in Reminders.

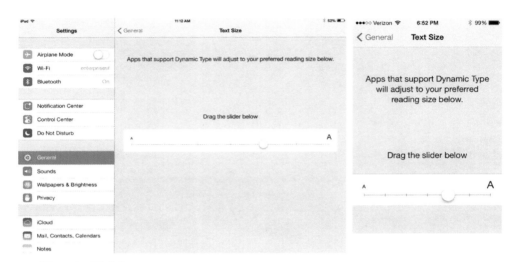

■ FIGURE 2-3

The new Text Size slider controls the default text size in compatible apps.

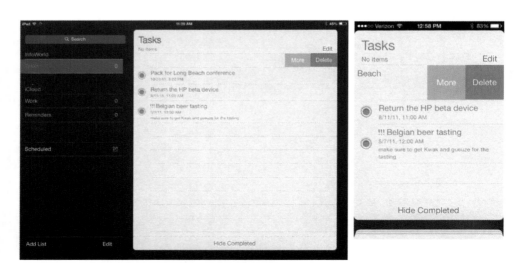

■ FIGURE 2-4

The Delete button for items in lists has a new look and a new companion: More.

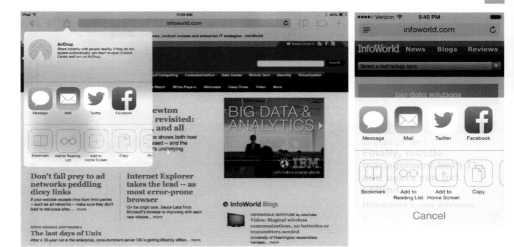

■ FIGURE 2-5

The Share sheet now segments its controls based on type.

Enhanced Sharing

The Share sheet has a new look, as Figure 2-5 shows. In addition to the visual simplification, the new Share sheet separates sharing services like Facebook from iOS controls like Copy and Print. The new AirDrop direct-sharing feature appears as well (covered in the next section). Rather than have multiple panes for icons, there's now a single pane you scroll horizontally through.

iOS 7 adds two photo-sharing sites — Flickr and Vimeo — to its repertoire of social networks, and thus to the Share sheet if you sign into their accounts. (Go to the Settings app and look for the Flickr and Vimeo panes in the application section to sign in.)

Sharing with AirDrop

If you use a Mac, you probably know what AirDrop is: a way to share files directly between Macs. You open a Finder window, select AirDrop in the Sidebar, wait for the list of other Macs that also have AirDrop open, then drag files to the icon of the Mac you want to send the files to. That person has to accept the AirDrop, and can send you files the same way, if you allow it.

AirDrop in iOS 7 works similarly. You share content, such as photos and Web links, using the Share sheet. But instead of choosing Mail or

Messages or some other app, you choose an iOS device in the AirDrop section of the Share sheet. That person is then asked whether to accept the AirDrop, which goes to the same app on that person's iOS device as it came from on yours: Photos in the Photos app go to the other person's Photos app, Web URLs go to Safari, and so on.

⊚ **Note**

AirDrop on the Mac and AirDrop in iOS do not work together. You cannot share content between iOS devices and Macs via AirDrop. AirDrop on the Mac works only with other Macs, and AirDrop in iOS works only with other iOS devices.

⊚ **Note**

AirDrop works only with newer iOS devices, just as it works on the Mac only with newer models (those with Lightning connectors). The reason is that it relies on specific functions that were included only in recent version of the Wi-Fi chip. If your device doesn't support AirDrop, you won't see it in your Share sheet or in Control Center.

AirDrop requires the recipient to agree to accept the content, so it can't be used to force or sneak content onto someone else's iOS device. But you can limit who can even ask to send you AirDropped content. To do so, open the Control Center, then tap the AirDrop button. A pop-over appears with three choices:

- **Everyone**, which lets anyone on the same Wi-Fi network see you in his or her Share sheets' AirDrop section.
- **Contacts Only**, which lets only people listed in your Contacts app ask to send you content. I recommend you set AirDrop to this setting, and change it to Everyone only when you are in a meeting or conference, when you can reasonably expect to get legitimate sharing requests from strangers.
- **Off**, which makes you invisible to everyone as far as AirDrop sharing goes.

Siri's Expanded Reach

Apple's Siri service gets a big improvement in iOS 7. First, Siri uses more of your screen to present results, so you can see more movie listings on the screen or see larger maps or restaurants you're seeking details on, for example, a Figure 2-6 shows.

Siri also searches more sources, so you'll get fewer "I didn't find anything for" responses in iOS 7. For example, Siri can now search Twitter and display tweets in its window, so you don't have to leave Siri to read them. And it can search Wikipedia and display the summary results without leaving Siri, while also letting you go to the Wikipedia website for more details as well as seek more information from suggested search engines, such as Bing and Wolfram Alpha, as Figure 2-7 shows.

Tip

You can now choose a male or female voice for Siri. Do so in the Settings app's General pane, in its Siri controls.

■ FIGURE 2-6

Siri provides more information on its screen than before, by using a full-screen overlay rather than a pop-over to display results.

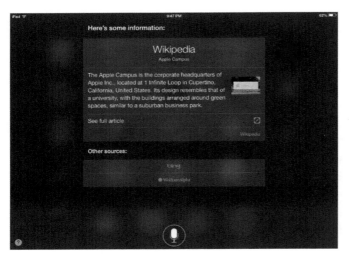

■ FIGURE 2-7

Siri now provides summarizes Wikipedia entries, as well as lets you explore the description more fully in Safari at Wikipedia or from other search engines.

Contacts

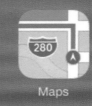
Reminders

Maps

Video

Camera

Photo Booth

Photos

Game Ce

Messages

Clock

App Store

iTunes S

Calculator

The
Weather
Channel

TWC

Find Friends

FaceTi

• • • • • • •

Friday
9

⬜

iCloud and
Photo Stream

Cloud is an addictive syncing service, automatically keeping photos, music, documents, keyboard shortcuts, Safari bookmarks, reminders, and now passwords automatically up to date across your Apple devices — Macs and iOS devices — that are signed into the same iCloud account.

In iOS 7, iCloud works as it did before, using the same controls in the Settings app's iCloud pane to specify what apps sync via iCloud, as well as to manage your iCloud storage and backups.

Syncing Passwords and Credit Cards

But iOS 7 adds a new kind of iCloud syncing called iCloud Keychain. A keychain is a set of stored passwords that the system remembers for you — it's like carrying a set of keys: If you have the keychain, you have all the keys, which in this case are passwords. You set up iCloud Keychain in the Settings app's iCloud pane.

After you turn on the iCloud Keychain switch, you'll be asked to enter your iCloud password, then enter the iCloud Keychain PIN you set up when you first signed into iCloud Keychain (usually done on your Mac or PC, via the iCloud system preference or iCloud control panel), and then wait for a text message to appear in the Messages app with a

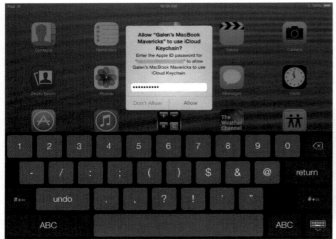

☐ FIGURE 3-1

If you disable iCloud Keychain and then re-enable it, you'll need to provide your iCloud password to confirm your device is allowed access to synced passwords and credit cards.

one-time security code. That's right: You need to enter three passwords to enable iCloud Keychain. After all, once enabled, your device now has all your synced passwords and credit card information saved in Safari on any of your devices. (If you use iCloud Keychain for the first time on an iOS device, you'll be taken through a series of screens in which you create that PIN and confirm your identity.)

But once you've enabled iCloud Keychain, you don't have to enter those credentials again, unless you turn off iCloud Keychain and then turn it back on later. If you do, you'll need to re-enter your iCloud password, as Figure 3-1 shows.

◯ Caution

If you use iCloud Keychain, be sure to password-protect your iOS device. Otherwise, a thief will be able to use your stored passwords and credit cards. Even if you don't use iCloud Keychain, a thief has access to your contacts, e-mail, and much more, so using a password is a good idea regardless.

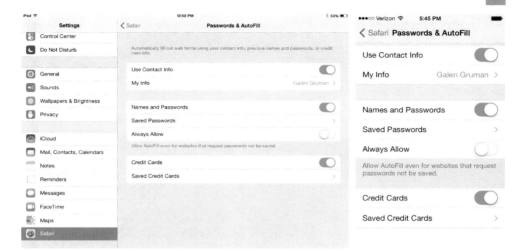

■ FIGURE 3-2

You can manage your saved passwords and credit cards in the Settings app's Safari pane, using the Password & AutoFill controls.

◎ Tip

You can manage what's stored in iCloud Keychain in Safari on your iOS device, Mac, or PC. On an iOS device, go to the Settings app's Safari pane and go to the Password & AutoFill controls, shown in Figure 3-2. On a computer, go to the AutoFill pane in the Preferences dialog box to add, delete, and rename saved information.

Once iCloud Keychain is enabled, any passwords or credit card numbers you choose to save in Safari on any of your devices are made available to the rest of your devices. When you enter a password or credit card number for the first time in Safari, you'll be asked whether you want to save it. (As a safety precaution, Safari and iCloud Keychain do not save your credit card's CVV number, a three- or four-digit code imprinted on the card that most websites require you enter to provide you actually have the card with you.)

Automatic App Updating

Another new iCloud feature is automatic updates, which comes in two forms in iOS 7.

□ **FIGURE 3-3**
Automatic updates are now an option in iOS 7.

The first form is to have apps automatically update themselves, so you don't have to open the App Store app when updates become available and tap Update All. In the Settings app's iTunes & App Store pane, set the Updates switch to On, as shown in Figure 3-3, to have apps update themselves without your intervention.

○ **Tip**

I strongly suggest that you set the Use Cellular Data switch to Off on your iPhone and any cellular iPads, so you don't burn through your data plan on app updates. If this switch is off, updates to your music, books, and apps will occur only when you are connected to the Internet via a Wi-Fi network. (If you have an unlimited data plan, then by all means use that data!)

Just remember: If you set up automatic updates, you can't choose which apps updates. They all will. So if a developer makes an app worse, you're stuck with it. Even if you reinstall an old version via iTunes from your Mac's Time Machine backup, the new version will automatically override that reinstalled old version.

The other form of automatic update is automatic content updating. Before iOS 7, only one app at a time could run unfettered, and when you switched to a different app, the other apps essentially were made to

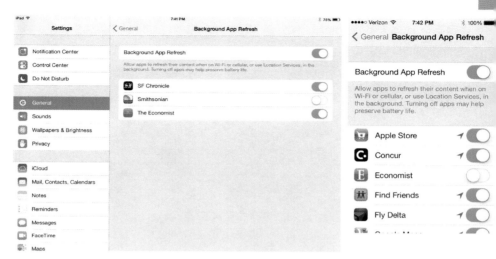

◼ FIGURE 3-4

You can specify which apps, if any, update their content when running in the background.

sleep, except for a few services like music playback and notifications that Apple let all apps use even while asleep. iOS 7 now offers what's called multitasking, meaning that apps continue to run full-bore even when not displayed onscreen — just like a PC or Mac app does.

That means that apps can keep their content updated and access Location Services to keep track of your current location even when you're not viewing them, such as navigation or news apps. But that constant background refreshing can use battery life and of course it consumes data, so you may want to disable automatic content updating for all apps or for just specific apps. You do so in the Settings app's General pane, using the Background App Refresh options shown in Figure 3-4.

To disable background content updates for all apps, set the Background App Refresh switch to Off. If the switch is set to On, you can specify which apps update in background using their specific switches.

FIGURE 3-5
You can specify which apps, if any, update their content when running in the background.

> **◯ Note**
>
> If an app uses Location Services, you'll see the location icon (the blue arrowhead) next to its switch if the switch is set to On. Remember you can control which apps can track your location in the Settings app's Privacy pane, using the individual switches for each app in the Location Services settings.

Enhancements to Photo Stream

The Photos app gets a new, streamlined look with a new way of looking at your photos, as Chapter 5 explains. But there's also a change in the iCloud-powered Photo Stream feature, now labeled Shared Streams in the Photos app. That is the new Activity screen, which displays in streams list when you tap the Shared button to see thumbnails of all the Photo Streams you've created or have joined.

Go to the Activity screen to see all images shared by everyone whose Photo Streams you've subscribed to. It's essentially a unified photo inbox for all your Photo Streams, as Figure 3-5 shows.

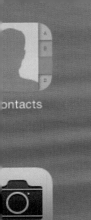
ontacts

Reminders

Maps

Videos

Camera

Photo Booth

Photos

Game Cer

essages

Clock

App Store

iTunes St

Calculator

TWC

Find Friends

FaceTim

● ● ● ● ● ● ● ●

Friday
9

Communications Apps

Although not as touted as other iOS 7 features, there are several new capabilities in the Phone, FaceTime, Messages, Mail, and Safari apps that make your iOS device a better communicator. New controls also help you better manage your cellular data usage.

The Phone App

The Phone app has three new features. One is the ability to block unwanted callers. As more of us use just a cell phone as our telephone, telemarketers and other abusive callers become a big problem. After all, we tend to have our iPhones with us 24/7, so interruptions follow us 24/7. And if your cellular plan charges you for buckets of voice minutes, those spam calls essentially steal the minutes you've paid for

In the U.S., it's illegal for telemarketers to call cell phones, but many do. Plus, there's a big loophole: If you give your number to a business, such as your bank or credit card agency, they can call you on that number for any purpose, which means legal spam in addition to legitimate calls such as to verify transactions. Short of giving all businesses a fax number or a fake number and risking not getting notices of potentially fraudulent transactions, you're basically stuck giving out your cell number.

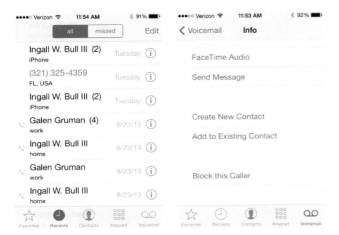

■ FIGURE 4-1

Tap the Details button (the **i** icon) in the Phone app (at left) to open the Details screen (at right) then scroll down and tap Block This Caller.

iOS can help lessen the pain by letting you block callers. When you get unwanted calls, you can block them, so they can't call your iPhone again. To do so, tap the Details button (the **i** icon) to the right of the unwanted phone number or contact name in the Phone app's Recents or Voicemail panes, then scroll to the bottom of the Details screen that appears and tap Block This Caller, as Figure 4-1 shows. (You can unblock a caller the same way; the Block This Caller label will read Unblock This Caller if you previously blocked that number or person.)

You can also manage blocked callers — view, add, or delete them — in the Settings app's Phone pane. Tap the Blocked option to get a list of blocked callers and the Add New button to block people stored in the Contacts app (all numbers listed for that person will be blocked). To unblock a caller, flick to the left over the name or number and tap the Unblock button that appears, as shown in Figure 4-2.

The second new feature in the Phone app is the ability to display pictures of the people in your Favorites pane, as Figure 4-3 shows. The photos are automatically added for each contact in the Contacts app with a photo. Given that Contacts can sync with Facebook, Twitter, and various contact services such as Google Contacts, chances are that you have photos of many people in Contacts.

If you don't want photos to appear in the Favorites pane, go to the Settings app's Phone pane and set the Contact Photos in Favorites switch to Off.

■ **FIGURE 4-2**
You can manage blocked callers in the Settings app's Phone pane, using the Blocked controls.

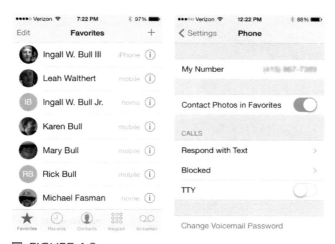

■ **FIGURE 4-3**
Tap the Details button (the **i** icon) in the Phone app (at left) to open the details screen (at right) then scroll down and tap Block This Caller.

The third new feature in the Phone app is the ability to respond to an incoming call with a text message. In addition to the Answer and Decline buttons, the Phone app may now display the Text and Remind Me buttons as well, which lets you reply via a text message or set a reminder to call that person, respectively. If you respond with a text, a menu of predefined text messages appears. You set these in the Settings app's Phone pane using the Respond with Text controls. If you set a reminder, you get options such as an hour later or when you get home. Note that Remind Me button doesn't appear if a person isn't in your Contacts app, and the Text button doesn't appear if the caller isn't using a cell phone.

The FaceTime App

Just as you can block unwanted callers in the Phone app, you can do block unwanted callers in the FaceTime app. The process is the same as for the Phone app; likewise, you use the Settings app's FaceTime pane to you manage blocked callers in the Settings app's Phone pane to manage blocked callers.

Like the Phone app, the FaceTime app also displays photos of any contacts in its Favorites pane. On an iPhone, you can disable the photo display by setting the Contact Photos in Favorites switch to Off in the Settings app's Phone pane; there's no equivalent control on an iPad.

And FaceTime has a new mode called FaceTime Audio, for conducting audio chats with other FaceTime users. When you initiate a FaceTime call, you're now asked whether you want a standard (video) call or an audio-only call. Likewise, you'll see both the standard FaceTime video-camera icon ( ) and the new FaceTime Audio phone icon ( ) in Contacts to choose what kind of FaceTime chat you want to start.

The Messages App

Just as you can block unwanted callers in the Phone app, you can do block unwanted texters in the Messages app. The process is the same as for the Phone app, and you use the Settings app's Messages pane to manage blocked texters the same way you use Settings app's Phone pane to manage blocked callers.

Managing Cellular Data

iOS 7 gives you control over which apps can use cellular data, to help you from exceeding your plan's limits. Go to the Settings app's Cellular pane — now a top-level pane, not a control within the General pane — and scroll down to get a list of apps that access the Internet. Next to each app is a switch that lets you control whether that app sends or receives data over a cellular connection, as Figure 4-4 shows.

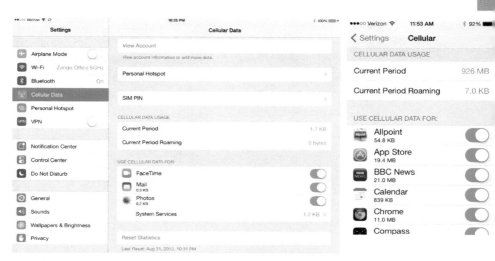

FIGURE 4-4

Use the Cellular pane in the Settings app to control which apps can use cellular data.

The Cellular pane in Settings also now shows how much data you've used during the current billing period, so you can more easily track your usage and adjust how much data you're using if necessary.

The Mail App

When you flick to the left on a message in the message list, the Trash button (previously called Delete) has a new companion button: More. Tap More to get quick access to the options you previously had available only within a message — Reply, Forward, Flag, Mark as Unread, and Move Message —as well as a new option: Move to Junk. Figure 4-5 shows the button and the pop-over that appear with those options.

The Move to Junk option is a nice addition, as it keeps your trash clear of obvious junk, making it easier to retrieve accidentally deleted messages.

Mail finally addresses an omission that has annoyed users for years: the inability to mark all messages as read. In iOS 7, when you tap Edit at the top of the message list and don't select any messages, the Mark option at the bottom of the message list displays as Mark All, as Figure 4-6 shows. Tap Mark All to get the two options: Mark as Read and Flag. Now, you can deal with all the messages in an inbox or folder in one fell swoop. But what you can't do is delete all those messages; you still have to delete the messages by tapping their selection bubbles and then tapping Trash.

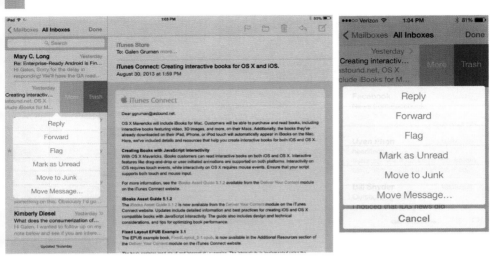

■ FIGURE 4-5

The new More button for e-mail messages gives you quick access to common controls from the message list, as well as the new Move to Junk option.

A subtle change in Mail is the addition of smart folders, folders whose contents are based on rules, such as unread messages or those with attachments. You can't create your own rules, such as the Mac's Mail app lets you do, but at least you can select from canned rules in iOS 7.

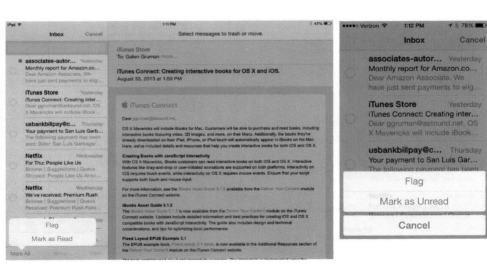

■ FIGURE 4-6

If you tap Edit but select no e-mails, the Mark All option appears in iOS 7's Mail app.

Note

When you select multiple messages, the flick gesture is not available. Instead, you use the Mark, Move, and Trash buttons at the bottom of the message list, as in previous iOS versions. (To select multiple items. tap Edit at the top of the message list to display the selection bubbles next to each message, then tap the selection bubbles for each message you want to act on, then tap the button at the bottom of the list for the desired action.)

iOS 6 offered the VIP smart mailbox, as well as the Flagged smart mailbox. iOS 7 adds:

- **To or CC**, which doesn't show messages that you were blind-copied (BCC'd) on.
- **Attachments**, which shows only messages that contain attachments, so you no longer have to hunt for them.
- **All Drafts**, which shows all messages in your e-mail accounts Drafts folders, so you no longer can easily get to them.
- **All Sent**, which shows you all messages you've sent from all accounts.
- **All Trash**, which shows you all deleted messages in all accounts (excluding messages in the Junk folders).

■ FIGURE 4-7

The Mail app now supports several smart folders, for easier access to messages based on their predefined rules. You can also put commonly used folders in the Mailboxes list.

You choose which smart mailboxes to display by going to the Mailboxes view (see Figure 4-7) and tapping Edit. Select the smart mailboxes you want to display in the Mailboxes list, and use the reorder handles to arrange them to your preferred order. Deselect any smart mailboxes that you don't want in the Mailboxes list. Tap Done when you've adjusted the smart mailboxes' display to your liking.

In addition, you can now add folders from your e-mail accounts to the Mailboxes list in Mail by tapping Add Mailbox. This way, you can quickly go to a commonly used folder without first having to open the specific account from the Accounts list below the Mailboxes list and then navigating to that folder from there.

Another subtle change is how mailbox search works. As before, drag down at the top of the message list to expose the Search bar. After a few moments, you'll see two tabs at the top of the results: All Mailboxes and Current Mailbox. Tap All Mailboxes to expand your search.

If you use multiple e-mail accounts, Mail remembers the account you last used to send e-mail to that person, and sets your From account accordingly for that person (you can change it in the message, of course).

And when you enter a person's name in the To, Cc, or Bcc field, Mail now lists not only matching people but on-the-fly groups you frequently send e-mails that include that person. For example, entering "Tom" will show all Toms plus "Tom, Dick, and Mary" if you often send e-mails to all three at the same time.

The Safari Browser

Using the iCloud Keychain feature, the Safari browser can now save and sync credit card information and sync them and passwords with Safari on your Macs, PCs, and other iOS devices, as Chapter 3 explains. And it can share URLs, photos, and other content from websites via AirDrop and the photo-sharing sites Flickr and Vimeo, as Chapter 2 explains.

But Safari has other cool new features as well. One is Shared Links, which displays all links sent to your social media accounts, such as Twitter and Facebook. Shared Links is essentially a special bookmark list. You access the list via the Bookmarks button, as Figure 4-8 shows. Tap the Shared List button (the @ icon) to see each shared link with the social network's icon and the description of the link. That description acts as a link; tap it to open its Web page.

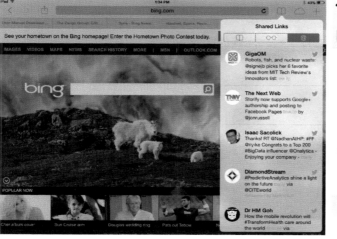

■ FIGURE 4-8

Safari's Shared Links bookmarking provides one place for all Web pages shared to you via your social networks.

Not so much new but different is how iOS 7's Safari handles searching. There are no longer separate URL and Search bars. They're combined into one, as Figure 4-9 shows. Tap the combined bar to enter

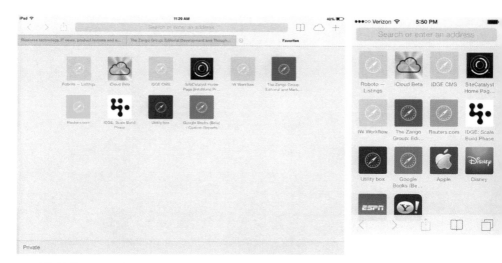

■ FIGURE 4-9

The new Favorites pane shows thumbnail icons for each Web page you've bookmarked as a favorite.

☐ FIGURE 4-10
The new look of the iPhone's browser tabs in Safari

a URL or to search. If there's a URL already there, don't worry: When you tap the bar, the entire string is selected, so whatever you type replaces it.

Also, when you tap the URL and Search bar, the Favorites pane opens, as Figure 4-9 shows, listing any websites you've marked as a favorite. You mark a Web page as a favorite by tapping the Share button, tapping Bookmarks, and choosing Favorites in the Location menu — that's a new option for bookmarks. Any favorites designated in Safari on your Mac, PC, or other iOS devices sync across all your devices, so they will appear in the Favorites pane as well.

 Tip

If you want another set of bookmarks to open in a new browser tab instead of Favorites, you can choose that set in the Settings app's Safari pane, using the Favorites options.

 Tip

You can display the favorites in their own bar, below the URL and Search bar, just like Safari works in OS X and Windows. Go to the Settings app's Safari pane and use the Show Favorites Bar switch to do so.

And when you tap the New Tab button (the + icon), the new tab automatically displays your favorites, under the assumption that you may want one of those Web pages, so why not make them immediately available?

The iPhone version of Safari also has a striking new look for showing open Web pages. Gone are the horizontally arranged preview windows that you scroll through sideways. New is the set of vertically stacked windows shown in Figure 4-10 (very similar to how the Google Chrome browser works for smartphones) that you scroll through up and down.

◯ Note

You still close browser tabs the same way: by tapping the Close button (the X icon). On the iPhone, you can also drag out a tab to close it.

iOS 7's Safari no longer has an eight-tab limit for open Web pages. You can open an infinite number. On the iPad, press the **...** button that appears to the right of the tabs to get a pop-over of additional tabs. On the iPhone, just keep scrolling.

A small change is that the Reader label has changed to an icon (≡) in the URL and Search bar. Tap it to see a stripped-down version of the Web page, with ads, navigation, and other peripheral content removed so you can focus on just the article you are reading. (The Reader feature is not available for all websites, and the icon will not appear if a site doesn't support it.)

Finally, you can switch to Private Browsing mode at any time by tapping the Private button. (You no longer have to go to the Settings app's Safari pane.) This mode disables the history feature, so your visit to the page is not recorded. To get the Private button on an iPad, tap the URL and Search bar; the Private button appears at bottom of the Safari screen. On an iPhone, scroll to the top of the page, then tap the Tabs button (the ⊓ icon) to display the open browser tabs; the Private button displays at the bottom of the screen.

There are several new privacy settings in the Safari pane of the Settings app as well. You can enable the Do Not Track feature that some websites honor, and you can disable the Smart Search capability's top hits and suggestions features, both of which rely on tracking your website visits to make the suggestions.

ntacts

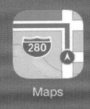

Reminders

Maps

Videos

amera

Photo Booth

Photos

Game Cent

ssages

Clock

App Store

iTunes Sto

culator

TWC

Find Friends

FaceTime

Friday

9

Photography Apps

The iPhone is the top source of photos on the Web, or so Apple claims. It's likely true, given how many people use their iPhone's built-in camera to snap photos. iOS 7's integration with Facebook, Twitter, Flickr, and Vimeo makes it very easy to share those photos with friends and family over the Web, and of course Apple's own Photo Stream technology (see Chapter 3) lets you share photos with others and sync your photos across your Mac, PC, and iOS devices.

iOS 7 makes some big changes to the two photography apps that come with iPhones and iPads: There's a very different user interface in the Photos app, and the Camera app has new a option when taking photos.

The Photos App for Managing Photos

When you open the Photos app, you no longer see in the Photos pane the grid of photos you've shot on your iOS device. Instead, you see the groups of photo tiles grouped by year, date range, or date. Essentially, you can zoom in or out in time, seeing all photos in the selected time frame.

The Years view, shown in Figure 5-1, shows all your photos for every year. Tap any image in the Years view to narrow down the time scale

■ FIGURE 5-1

The Years view in the Photos app

■ FIGURE 5-2

The Collections view in the Photos app

to a week or two around when that image was taken, in what is called Collections view, shown in Figure 5-2. Tap a photo in the Collections view to zoom in time yet again, to what is called Moments view, shown in Figure 5-3, which organizes photos by day. (The Moments view replaces the Events pane in prior iOS versions' Photos app.)

■ FIGURE 5-3

The Moments view in the Photos app

◯ **Tip**

In Years and Collections views, tap and hold a specific photo to see only that photo in full frame. In Moments view, just tap the photo to see it in full frame.

◯ **Tip**

In Moments view, the Share button appears. Tap it to get two options: Share This Moment, which selects all photos for that moment, and Share Some Photos, which opens a grid of that moment's photos for you to select the ones you want to share. Either way, you get the standard Share sheet where you select how you want to share the photos.

You can zoom back out by tapping Collections in the Moments view, or by tapping Years in the Collections view.

You probably noticed the location names above each group of photos in all three views. Tap it to open a map that shows where the photos were taken, as Figure 5-4 shows. To open a grid of photos taken at a specific location, tap the sample photo at that location. (This ability replaces the Places pane in prior iOS versions' Photos app.)

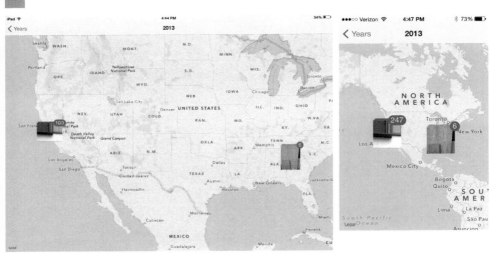

■ FIGURE 5-4

The new view of photos by location in iOS 7

The rest of the Photos app works as it did before, even if the look is a bit different. You manage your Photo Streams in the Shared pane (which had been called the Photo Stream pane), and you manage your albums in the Album pane using the same methods as before.

Well, there are two differences.

First, as noted in Chapter 3, there's the new Activity view for Shared Photo Streams that shows all your subscribed streams' photos in one place.

Second, if you open a Shared Photo Stream, you'll see a new button: People. Tap it to change the sharing settings, such as to invite others to subscribe to the Shared Photo Stream, to allow subscribers to post their own photos to the stream, to control whether the stream is available on the Web for anyone to see, to specify whether you get notifications as to new posts, and to delete a stream. Figure 5-5 shows the screens.

You could do those actions in prior versions of iOS — except change posting permissions after a stream had been shared, which is new to iOS 7 — but it was not so obvious how (you had to tap Edit in the Photo Stream pane, then tap an album, and then change the settings in the Edit Photo Stream dialog box that opened).

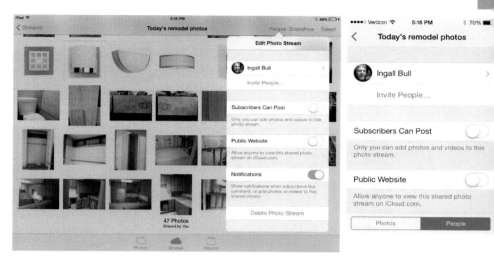

FIGURE 5-5

The new People button opens the revamped controls for editing Shared Photo Stream settings.

The Camera App

iOS 7 adds one new feature when shooting pictures: the Square option to take photos that are square, rather than rectangular. Square photos are common on websites, so this option lets you avoid the effort of later on cropping Web-destined photos to be square.

The interface for the Camera app has also changed a little, as Figure 5-6 shows.

On the iPad, all the controls are now in a single overlay bar on the right side of the screen: Select Camera, HDR On/Off, Photograph (or Start/Stop if you're shooting video), and the shooting modes (Video, Photo, Square, and, if supported by your device, Pano), as well as the icon to open the Camera Roll in the Photos app.

On the iPhone, there's an overlay bar at the top for the flash, HDR, and camera-selection controls, and there's an overlay bar at the bottom for the Photograph or Start/Stop button, the shooting modes, and the Camera Roll.

You change shooting modes not by tapping the desired mode but by sliding the modes as if they were on a dial, so the desired mode lines up with the yellow selector icon adjacent to them (see Figure 5-6).

■ FIGURE 5-6

The Camera app reworks the user interface for the mostly familiar controls. Gone is the Grid control, and new is the Square photo option.

Zooming works as it did in previous versions of iOS: Use the familiar standard pinch and expand gestures, or use the slider that appears once you begin pinching or expanding. Also as before, tap on the screen to set the focal point.

◯ **Note**

To take a photo when not using the Camera app, use the Control Center's Camera button. Chapter 1 explains the new Control Center.

What you won't see in the Camera app is the control for enabling or disabling the grid, which helps you align the camera so what you're shooting appears level. That control still exists, but you now have to set it in the Camera section of the Settings app's Photos & Camera pane.

Also in the Settings app's Photos & Cameras pane is a new control: Keep Normal Photo. If set to On, it keeps both a standard version and a high-dynamic-range (HDR) version of any photos you take when HDR is turned on. Saving HDR photos does take a bit more storage on your iOS device, but it also gives you the most flexibility when working on your photo in a program like iPhoto, Aperture, or Photoshop. There's rarely a reason to turn this off.

☐ FIGURE 5-7

The new Filters options let you apply predefined special effects to your photo in the Photos app.

The Photos App for Editing Photos

You take photos in the Cameras app, but you edit them in the Photos app (or an independent app like iPhoto or Snapseed). When viewing a photo in your Camera Roll or other album in Photos, tap Edit to get the editing controls. iOS 7 keeps the red-eye removal, cropping/straightening, rotation, and auto-enhancement tools you already have and adds a new tool called Filters.

The Filters tool provides eight predefined filters to change the color profile of the photo, as if you used a special filter on the camera lens: Mono, Tonal, Noir, Fade, Chrome, Process, Transfer, and Instant. Figure 5-7 shows the filters. Tap a filter to apply it, and keep tapping on filters until you see an effect you like — or tap Cancel to leave the photo untouched.

 Tip

If you later decide you don't like the filter effect, edit the photo in Photos and tap the None filter. The filter effect is gone!

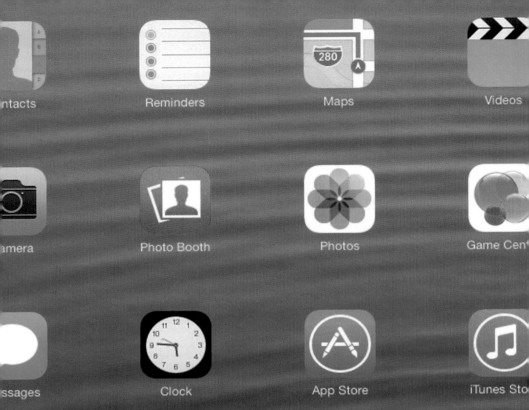

ntacts
Reminders
Maps
Videos

amera
Photo Booth
Photos
Game Cen

ssages
Clock
App Store
iTunes Sto

culator
TWC
Find Friends
FaceTim

Friday
9

Other Apps and Services

There are of course lots of small changes across iOS 7 and its apps, beyond the bigger changes covered earlier in this book. This chapter highlights those other changes.

Changes in Other Apps

In addition to the visual differences due to iOS 7's new user interface, several applications have new or changed functionality.

App Store

The new Near Me pane shows apps popular with other people in your vicinity. Yes, it's a gimmick meant to drive more app sales.

The more meaningful change is the ability for iOS 7 to update apps automatically, as described in Chapter 3.

Clock

The Clock app's home-screen icon now shows the current time — even the second hand's movements are accurate.

Maps

You'll see the Share button in the Maps app when viewing directions or a location. That means you can now share that destination or location with others via AirDrop or a social site. You use the same Share sheet to bookmark directions as well.

A bigger deal is the ability to received directions from a Mac running OS X Mavericks' Maps app. You can send yourself directions from your computer so your iPhone or cellular iPad is ready to navigate. The sent directions display in the Maps app on your iOS device, and also remain available in the Maps app's bookmarks.

In the Settings app's Maps pane, you can now choose to make either driving directions or walking directions your preferred directions type. Maps will display directions based on that preference, but you can always choose a different type for the current directions within the Maps app. Also, the Label Size choice for Maps in the Settings app are gone; Maps bases its label size on the new Text Size control covered in Chapter 2.

Music

Apple's been promoting heavily its new iTunes Radio service, which streams music from your choice of genres to your iPhone or iPad, with the periodic commercials — just like old-fashioned radio. You'll see featured radio stations at the top of the screen when you go to the Music app's Radio pane, as well as any favorites you added in the My Stations list below the featured stations, as Figure 6-1 shows.

To add a station, tap the Add button (the + icon), choose the desired stations from the lists that appear, and tap the circle to the right of their names to confirm the selection. To play a radio "station," tap it in the Radio pane.

iTunes Radio displays a price button for a song as it plays, to encourage you to buy your own copy. And you can pause a song as it plays.

 **Caution**

Streaming audio over a cellular connection can eat up your data plan's allotment.

■ FIGURE 6-1

iTunes Radio is a new option in the Music app.

For some time, Apple's iTunes for Macs and Windows PCs has had the notion of shared libraries, where content stored on a computer can be listened to or watched by someone else on the Wi-Fi network, if signed in to the same Home Sharing account. With the free Remote app from Apple, iOS devices could also access these shared libraries.

Now, for iPads at least, you don't need that separate app: the new Shared pane in the iPad's Music app lets you open a shared library and play it from the standard iOS player. (If you don't see this option, tap the More button at the bottom of the Music app's screen.) Figure 6-3 later in this chapter shows the equivalent feature in the Videos app.

Passbook

The iPhone-only Passbook app is a wonderful way to keep affinity cards, travel tickets, and entertainment tickets all available in one place — on your iPhone. You don't need to find a printer at your hotel, for example, to print your airline ticket, nor do you need to keep all those store cards in your wallet.

But sometimes, you have a paper ticket. Passbook can't handle those. Or at least it couldn't before iOS 7. Now there's the Scan Code button at the top of the Passbook screen that lets you use the iPhone's camera to scan in a bar code and convert it into a digital copy stored in the Passbook app.

■ FIGURE 6-2

Passbook can now scan bar codes to create a digital copy — but only for scan codes registered by their issuers.

However, this feature only works with printed bar codes that are linked to Passbook by whoever issued them, so you can't use it for just any printed tickets. Passbook will tell you when it can't use a scanned code, as Figure 6-2 shows.

Settings

In addition to the capabilities covered elsewhere in this book, the Settings app has the following changes:

■ iTunes Wi-Fi Sync now lets you sync your iOS device with more than one computer. Use the iTunes Wi-Fi Sync control in the General pane to select the computer you want to back up to. Any computer on the network using your Apple ID is available. This way, you can have multiple backups, such as one at your primary home and one in your vacation home. (When you attach an iOS device to your computer, you'll be asked whether to trust that computer; tap Trust to let that computer's iTunes manage and back up your device.)

■ The Brightness and Wallpaper pane is now called Wallpapers & Brightness.

■ The Picture Frame pane is gone; iOS no longer lets you use your lock screen as a picture frame to play a slideshow of photos from a selected album in the Photos app.

■ FIGURE 6-3

The Videos app on an iPad, like the Music app, can now access shared libraries from iTunes on your Mac or PC over the Wi-Fi network.

■ In the Mail, Contacts, Calendars pane, the new Short Name controls for contacts lets you specify whether short names are enabled and if so how they are created (First Name is the default). The Short Names feature lets iOS use a short name rather than a full name to save space when useful in a list or other onscreen display.

■ Also in the Mail, Contacts, Calendars pane, there's a new option to set which day of the week is the first day in the Calendar app's Weeks view.

■ In the Notes pane, gone is the option to set the default font. Notes now uses iOS 7's standard font, Helvetica Neue.

Videos

Just as the Music app on an iPad can now access shared libraries directly, so can the Videos app. Tap the Shared button to get a list of available libraries, then tap the libraries whose content you want to play on your iPad. After a few moments, you'll see their contents in the Videos app, ready to play over the Wi-Fi network on your tablet, as Figure 6-3 shows.

☐ FIGURE 6-4

The Weather app now shows the weather for all the cities you've selected for tracking (at left). Tap a city to get the full details (at right).

Weather

The iPhone's Weather app lets you track the weather in as many cities as you'd like, in addition to showing the weather forecast for wherever you are. In previous versions of iOS, you could see only one city's weather at a time. iOS 7 changes that: Tap the Chooser button (the ☰ icon) to see all your tracked cities at once, as Figure 6-4 shows.

Tap a city to get the full weather details. You can continue to navigate among those detailed views by swiping horizontally — you don't have to go to the Chooser view to see another city's weather.

To add more cities, tap the Add button (the + icon) at the bottom of the screen. To delete a city, flick to the left over its entry to get the Delete button.

Changes in Security and Privacy

iOS 7 also strengthens both security and privacy settings.

Find My iPhone's device lock

The biggest change is that the Find My iPhone feature locks your device to your Apple ID, even if it is erased. That means if someone steals your iPhone, they can't reactivate it on a cellular network; the device will insist on being signed in with your Apple ID and password. You can even have the device display a message on the iPhone or iPad each time it's turned on that tells a user the device has been lost or stolen — even if the device was erased. That message should discourage sales of stolen iOS devices.

For iPads and iPod Touches, Find My iPhone also requires that an Apple ID and password be entered if the device is erased and someone tries to restore it to its defaults.

In fact, for all iOS devices, Find My iPhone won't let anyone reset the device until Find My iPhone is turned off, which requires entering the correct Apple ID and password for that device. Once the Apple ID and password are entered, the device can be reset, such as to give it to someone else. Best of all, other than turning on Find My iPhone in the Settings app's iCloud pane, there's nothing you need to do to take advantage of this new capability.

Privacy controls

iOS 7 also adds more controls over your privacy. The Privacy pane in the Setting app, for example, adds a control for the internal microphone that lets you see which apps have accessed the microphone and lets you block their access on an individual basis. Also, the first time any app tries to use the microphone, you're asked whether to allow it, so your iOS device can't be turned into a surreptitious eavesdropper.

The Privacy pane also adds the Advertising control from which you can limit ad tracking. This control existed prior to iOS 7, but was buried in the General pane's About options, so most people didn't know they could limit ads that track them.

I strongly urge you to review all the settings available in the Privacy pane and its various controls to make sure you're comfortable with what apps and websites can track about you and what information stored on your iOS device they can tap.

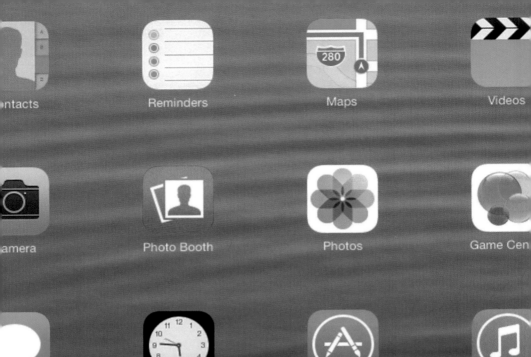

ntacts

Reminders

Maps

Videos

amera

Photo Booth

Photos

Game Cen

ssages

Clock

App Store

iTunes Sto

lculator

TWC

Find Friends

FaceTim

Friday
9

Index

Other Books by Galen Gruman

To buy, visit www.zangogroup.com/books.html

4597839R00042

Made in the USA
San Bernardino, CA
26 September 2013